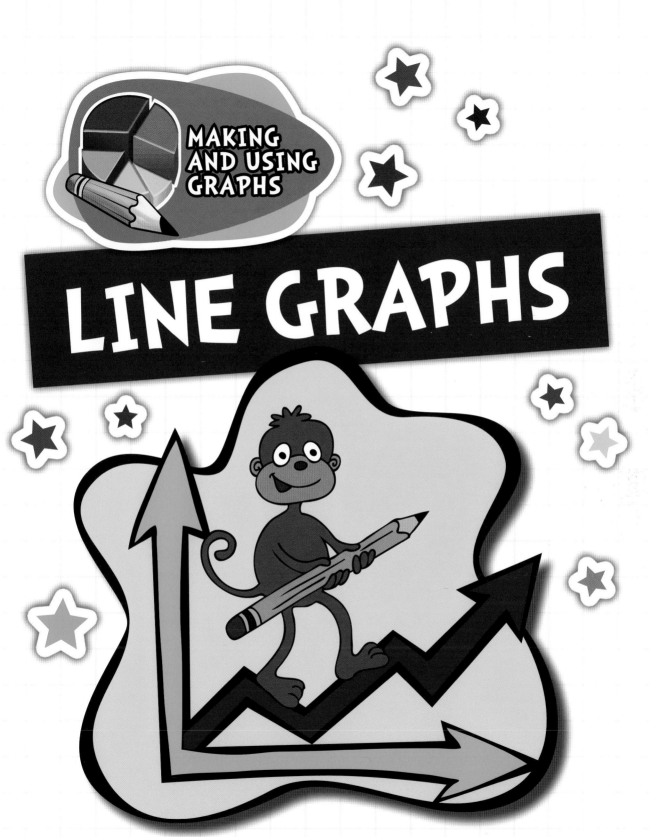

MAKING AND USING GRAPHS

LINE GRAPHS

by Lisa Colozza Cocca   illustrated by Kathleen Petelinsek

Published in the United States of America by Cherry Lake Publishing
Ann Arbor, Michigan
www.cherrylakepublishing.com

Consultants: Janice Bradley, PhD, Mathematically Connected Communities,
New Mexico State University; Marla Conn, Read-Ability

Editorial direction: Rebecca Rowell
Book design and illustration: The Design Lab

Photo credits: iStockphoto, 4; Jason Verschoor/iStockphoto, 8; Shutterstock
Images, 12, 20; Alexander Sysolyatin/Shutterstock Images, 16; Shutterstock
Images

Library of Congress Cataloging-in-Publication Data
Cocca, Lisa Colozza, 1957–
  Line graphs / Lisa Colozza Cocca.
    p. cm.
  Audience: 005-007
  Audience: Grades K to 3.
  Includes index.
  ISBN 978-1-61080-912-2 (hardback : alk. paper) – ISBN 978-1-61080-937-5
(paperback : alk. paper) – ISBN 978-1-61080-962-7 (ebook) –
ISBN 978-1-61080-987-0 (hosted ebook)
1. Mathematics—Graphic methods—Juvenile literature. 2. Graph theory—Juvenile
literature. I. Title.

  QA40.5.C629 2013
  511'.5—dc23

                        2012033982

Cherry Lake Publishing would like to acknowledge the work
of The Partnership for 21st Century Skills. Please visit
www.21stcenturyskills.org for more information.

Printed in the United States of America
Corporate Graphics Inc.
January 2013
CLFA10

Table of Contents

CHAPTER ONE

What Is a Line Graph?

We can use a line graph to track all kinds of things, including wait times for the roller coaster.

Have you ever measured something at different times to see how it changed? A line graph is a great way to easily compare numbers over time. A line graph is a type of number picture. If you want to see how many minutes people waited to ride the roller coaster throughout the day, a line graph can help. A line graph can help us understand sales at our lemonade stand, too.

Let's learn about line graphs! We'll start at the amusement park.

A line graph has many parts:

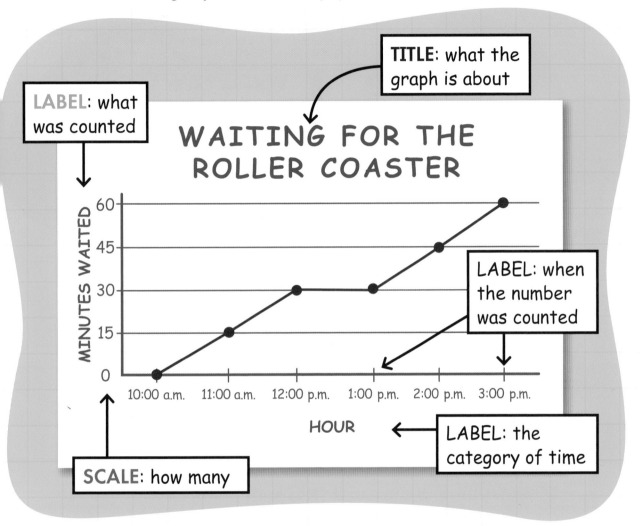

WAITING FOR THE ROLLER COASTER

MINUTES WAITED

60

45

30

15

0

10:00 a.m.   11:00 a.m.   12:00 p.m.   1:00 p.m.   2:00 p.m.   3:00 p.m.

HOUR

The points tell us how many minutes people waited to ride the roller coaster at different times of the day. The lines show us how the wait time changed during the day. When did people wait the longest? Was there a time when people didn't wait?

A line graph uses points to show amounts. Each point stands for a piece of **data**, or information. Lines connect the dots and show how the numbers change. When a line goes up, a number has increased. When a line goes down, a number has decreased. And when a line goes straight across, a number has stayed the same.

What kinds of things can we graph? Let's find out!

Here's what you'll need to complete the activities in this book:

- notebook paper
- pencil with an eraser
- ruler
- crayons or markers

Gather what you need.

CHAPTER TWO

Graphing Lemonade Sales

We can track our lemonade sales with a line graph.

Let's sell lemonade! We can use the money we make at the amusement park.

We can make a line graph to compare sales each day. First, we have to track how many cups of lemonade we sell. We can do that with a **tally chart**. To tally is to count. A tally chart is a great way to collect data for our graph.

Here's our tally chart:

LEMONADE SALES		
DAY	CUPS SOLD	TOTAL
Monday	IIII	4
Tuesday	JHT II	7
Wednesday	II	2
Thursday	JHT	5
Friday	JHT III	8
Saturday	JHT JHT II	12
Sunday	JHT JHT	10

The days we sold lemonade are listed in the left column. Each day has its own row. We make a **tally mark** for each cup we sell. The fifth **mark** goes across the other four.

Next, we count the tally marks in each row and write the numbers in the chart. Where should they go? Right! In the column labeled **Total**.

We're ready to make our line graph. We draw points on the graph to show the numbers. Next, we connect the points.

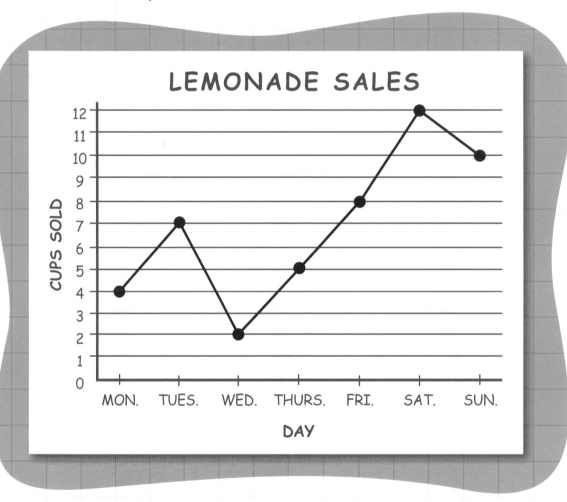

The lines show how the amount of lemonade we sold changed from day to day. How much lemonade did we sell Friday? Did the number go up or down from Saturday to Sunday?

Graph Drinking

Practice making a line graph. Record how much you drink each day for one week.

INSTRUCTIONS:
1. Use the tally chart on page 9 as a model for your chart.
2. Track the number of glasses of milk, juice, water, and other things you drink.
3. Use your data to make a line graph.
4. Draw dots or circles to show the number of glasses you drank each day.
5. Draw lines between the points to show how the number changed from day to day. If you want, use your ruler to help you draw straight lines.
6. Label the parts of your graph. Remember, the numbers go along the side. The days go along the bottom.
7. Give your graph a title.
8. Share your graph with a parent or friend.

To get a copy of this activity, visit www.cherrylakepublishing.com/activities.

CHAPTER THREE
Graphing Cows

On long driving trips through the countryside, counting cows can help pass the time.

Have you ever been on a long car trip? Let's pretend we're driving for hours through the country. We can count animals we see. Let's count cows!

Counting things can make the trip more fun. We can make a line graph to show how many cows we saw.

We counted cows for periods of five minutes every half hour. We used a tally chart to track how many cows we saw.

COWS WE SAW ON OUR TRIP		
WHEN WE COUNTED	NUMBER	TOTAL
Period 1	ЖЖ ЖЖ |||	13
Period 2	ЖЖ |||	8
Period 3	||	2
Period 4	ЖЖ		6
Period 5	||||	4
Period 6	ЖЖ ЖЖ	10

A tally chart is useful for tracking things as you count them.

The tally chart shows how many cows we saw during the different periods we counted. We can make a line graph with our data.

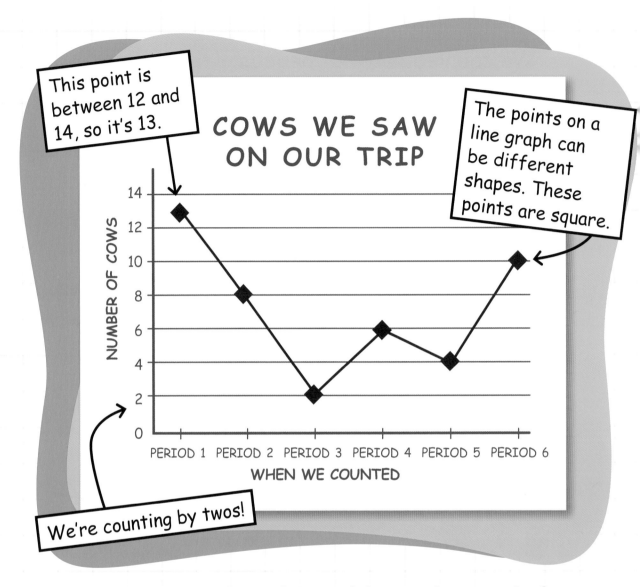

COWS WE SAW ON OUR TRIP

This point is between 12 and 14, so it's 13.

The points on a line graph can be different shapes. These points are square.

We're counting by twos!

The points show the total for each period of time we counted. Since we counted six times, we have six periods and six points.

What do the lines show us? That's right! We saw the most cows at the beginning and end of our trip.

Graph Cars

Practice making a line graph. Log how many cars you see at six different times.

INSTRUCTIONS:
1. Make a tally chart like the one on page 13.
2. Find a safe place to watch the street. Count the cars that pass by in five minutes six different times in one day. Try to count at least once in the morning, afternoon, and at night. Track your data in your tally chart.
3. Use your data to make a line graph. Your graph will have six points. The points will show how many cars you saw each time you counted.
4. Draw lines between the points.
5. Label the parts of your graph. Remember, the numbers go along the side. The periods when you counted go along the bottom.
6. Give your graph a title.
7. Share your graph with someone. Ask the person to tell you what it means.

To get a copy of this activity, visit www.cherrylakepublishing.com/activities.

CHAPTER FOUR

Graphing Clouds

Let's count clouds! We can track what we count in a line graph.

Sometimes, it's nice to lie on the ground and look at the sky. Let's do it! We can count the clouds that pass by while we're watching. We'll track the number of clouds we see in a chart and then make a line graph.

Here's our data. This time, instead of using tally marks, we just used numbers.

CLOUDS WE COUNTED	
DAY	NUMBER
Monday	3
Tuesday	4
Wednesday	10
Thursday	8
Friday	9
Saturday	4
Sunday	0

Here's our cloud data. Let's graph it!

Let's make a line graph. The chart shows we tracked clouds for seven days. How many points will be on our graph?

We put seven points on the graph. Next, we draw lines between the points. Why? That's right, to help us see how the numbers change over time.

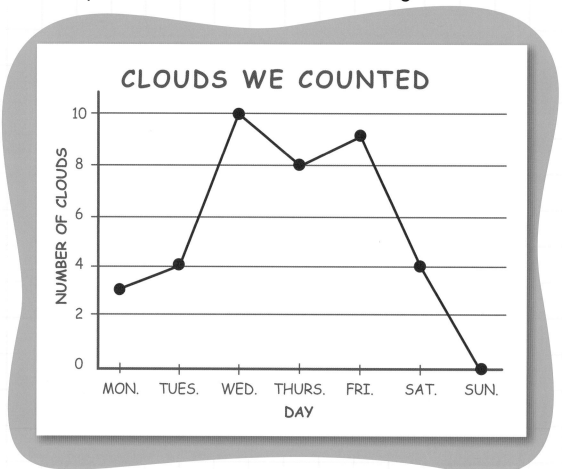

Look at our scale. We counted by twos. The point for Monday is between the lines for two and four. That means we saw three clouds on Monday. Did we see more clouds on Tuesday or on Thursday? Which day did we see the most clouds?

To get a copy of this activity, visit www.cherrylakepublishing.com/activities.

ACTIVITY

Graph Clouds

Practice making your own line graph about clouds.

INSTRUCTIONS:
1. Make a chart like the one on page 17.
2. Go out and look at the sky. How many clouds do you see? Write the number in your chart.
3. Count clouds one time every day for a week.
4. Use your data to make a line graph like the one on page 18. Copy the title, labels, and scale onto your graph.
5. Use the data from your chart to add points and lines.
6. What does your graph tell you? Which day did you see the most clouds? How many were there? Were there more clouds on Thursday or on Friday?
7. Show someone your graph. Ask him or her when you saw the most clouds and the least clouds.

CHAPTER FIVE

Line Graphs Are Fun

Line graphs are helpful for tracking change over time.

Using line graphs to see how things change is fun. Line graphs use points and lines to show data. They help us easily understand amounts and how they change over time. We can use them to compare the numbers of things. And we can see how something changes during a day, a week, or longer.

What else can you compare with a line graph? Keep practicing and find out!

Try showing other information with a line graph. Here are some ideas:

- Compare the amount of snow or rain that falls every day for one month.
- Record how many inches you grow during a year or from year to year.
- Find out how many minutes you watch TV each day for a week.
- Show the number of birthdays your class celebrates each month during the school year.

Line graphs are a great way to show how much you've grown.

Glossary

column (KAH-luhm) a line of data that goes from top to bottom

data (DAY-tuh) information recorded about people or things

label (LAY-buhl) a name; or to give something a name

row (roh) a line of data that goes from side to side

scale (skale) a series of numbers that shows how many

tally chart (TAL-ee chahrt) a way to record things you count that uses tally marks

tally mark (TAL-ee mahrk) a line that stands for one item of something being counted

title (TYE-tuhl) the name of a chart

total (TOH-tuhl) a sum; the amount after adding

For More Information

BOOKS

Lechner, Judith. *On the Trail with Lewis and Clark: Learning to Use Line Graphs*. New York: Rosen, 2003.

Murphy, Stuart J. *Less Than Zero*. New York: HarperCollins, 2003.

Piddock, Claire. *Line, Bar, and Circle Graphs*. New York: Crabtree, 2010.

WEB SITES

Kids' Zone: Learning with NCES—Create a Graph Classic, Line Graph
nces.ed.gov/nceskids/graphing/classic/line_data.asp
Make a line graph by typing in a title, labels, and data.

Math Is Fun—Data Graphs
www.mathsisfun.com/data/data-graph.php
Point and click to add your data to this graph. You can then show the same data as a bar graph, line graph, or pie graph.

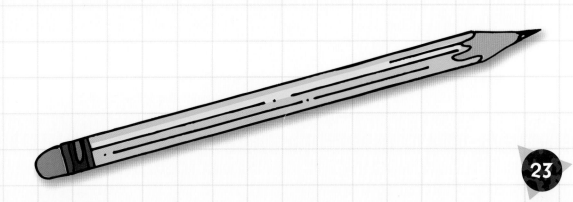

Index

About the Author

Lisa Colozza Cocca is a former teacher and school librarian. For the past decade, she has worked as a freelance writer and editor. She lives, works, and plays in New Jersey. Lisa thinks graphs are lots of fun.